Learning with

Text copyright © Claire Musters 2014
The author asserts the moral right
to be identified as the author of this work

Published by
The Bible Reading Fellowship
15 The Chambers, Vineyard
Abingdon OX14 3FE
United Kingdom
Tel: +44 (0)1865 319700
Email: enquiries@brf.org.uk
Website: www.brf.org.uk
BRF is a Registered Charity

ISBN 978 1 84101 695 5

First published 2014
10 9 8 7 6 5 4 3 2 1 0
All rights reserved

Acknowledgments
Unless otherwise stated, scripture quotations are taken from The Holy Bible, New International
Version® Anglicised, NIV® Copyright © 1979, 1984, 2011 by www.biblica.com, Biblica, Inc.®
Used by permission. All rights reserved worldwide.

Scripture quotations taken from the Contemporary English Version of the Bible, published by
HarperCollins Publishers, are copyright © 1991, 1992, 1995 American Bible Society.

Cover photo: iStockphoto/Thinkstock

Every effort has been made to trace and contact copyright owners for material used in this
resource. We apologise for any inadvertent omissions or errors, and would ask those concerned
to contact us so that full acknowledgment can be made in the future.

A catalogue record for this book is available from the British Library

Printed and bound by CPI Group (UK) Ltd, Croydon, CR0 4YY

Learning with  Foundations21
the new way to do discipleship

Prayer

A seven-week course of study material
for individuals and groups

Claire Musters

Dedication

I'd like to dedicate this book to my friends Naomi and Christine. As far as prayer goes, they are an inspiration to me. With their heart for people and love of God, prayer is as natural to them as their hearts' beating. They speak into people's lives, do battle on their behalf, intercede for them—and draw close to God in personal prayer, knowing that he is the source of all they do, say and are. They have motivated me to dig deep and learn how to cultivate both the discipline and the natural elements of my own prayer life.

Contents

Introduction

I wonder what comes into your mind when you think of the word 'prayer'. Is it an ongoing, vital communication with your God, a stale, boring discipline or something in between? As 21st-century Christians we face many challenges in trying to live out the Christian life, but we all have the same possibility of meeting the God we serve through prayer.

In 2013 the Church of England commissioned ICM Research to conduct a survey on prayer. The results of this survey indicated that many people believe in the power of prayer and said they would pray for such things as peace in the world, an end to poverty in the world, a family member and healing for another. In response to this, the Bishop of St Albans, the Rt Revd Dr Alan Smith, said, 'Prayer is one of the most natural and instinctive of human responses, so I am not surprised to see these findings. I come across people on an almost daily basis who want to talk about prayer and how to do it. This has been even more evident recently, as many people are facing uncertainty about jobs and finance. However, there has also been a desire to pray for trouble spots in the world, not least when we see the appalling photos from Syria on the television' (see www.churchofengland.org).

Prayer is a vital part of Christian discipleship. We are going to explore what prayer is, the example Jesus and other biblical characters set us for how to pray, ways to make it a part of our everyday lives and creative ideas on praying as individuals and together.

How to use this book

The book is divided into seven sections, each covering one week. Each week begins with a general introduction (Day 1), which is also the material for the group meeting (if you are working through this in a group setting) as you begin each new week together. This meeting can be at any time that suits your group. Around six to eight people are ideal, but you can decide what would work for your own particular group. You will need access to a computer for the meetings, as well as on the other days if at all possible, as there is sometimes online material to look up. If you are using a laptop, you can plug it into a domestic flat-screen TV for a larger picture.

It is best to have a group leader to ensure that the meetings keep on track. He or she can also take notes of discussions and remember to refer back to any challenge you agree to try out during the week, any thoughts that you may wish to look at again and/or any prayer requests that have been voiced. The details of this are up to you, as is the length of your group meeting, although I would suggest keeping it to one-and-a-half to two hours.

There are also optional daily sections for individual participants to read and ponder (Days 2–5). Each contains reflections/questions to work through. Ideally, each person should have access to a copy of this book. You may also find it beneficial to pair up so that you have someone to check progress with regularly throughout the seven weeks.

Finally, there are special Saturday and Sunday activities that are best done on those particular days. The Saturday section suggests a 'community' activity that you could do together (sometimes with others in your church/neighbourhood/workplace) and the one for Sunday is more of a reflective activity.

You may decide that your group meeting is best held on a Wednesday. You would therefore start with Day 1 on the Wednesday, with individual group members looking at Days 2 and 3 on their own. You would then break on the Saturday and Sunday to focus on those specific activities, then go back to complete Days 4 and 5 individually on the Monday and Tuesday before coming together again for the next group meeting the following Wednesday.

It is also possible, of course, simply to use the Day 1 group material, or to draw more flexibly from any of the material in the book. Another alternative is to use the Saturday 'community' material for a midweek meeting.

The material included in this book is based on BRF's Foundations21 website resource, which has 3500 pages of content and is organised into 'rooms' that cover different aspects of Christian discipleship. The material is arranged in four distinct pathways (Matthew, Mark, Luke and John) that represent different learning styles, so that each person can access the information in the learning style that best suits them. This book utilises material from each of the pathways to ensure that it is accessible to everyone. Every subject that is covered here can also be explored in further depth on the website (see www.foundations21.net) with particular reference to the 'Prayer' room.

A page for this book has been created on the Foundations21 website. This contains all the weblinks referenced in the book. Simply go to www.foundations21.net/prayer. Group activities for each Day 1 session can also be found here.

You do not need to be logged in to Foundations21 to view this page, but for further study it is worth registering with www.foundations21.net, which gives you full access to the website and is quick, easy and free.

Week 1
What is prayer?

Overview

Prayer teaches us to honour God. Through it, we learn how to be honest with him. We also discover how much we have to thank God for, and we start to learn the language of his love. By praying we become attuned to the needs of other people and the world around us. But what exactly *is* prayer?

Day 1 (group session)

Take a few moments to pray together before you begin this study.

Watch the video of prayer around the world: www.foundations21. net/prayer

Prayer has been called:

- work
- the Christian's 'vital breath'
- a divine hotline
- having my will aligned with God's

Question

How would you describe prayer?

Write your own definition of what prayer is and what it means to you. Share it with the group.

Group activity

Split into groups of three or four and take a look at these descriptions of prayer, some anonymous and others more famous quotations. Discuss which ones you like—or don't like—and explain why.

Prayer is an adventure of faith and trust.

Prayer can be long or short, happy or sad.

Prayer is expecting God to speak.

When I pray, coincidences happen; when I don't, they don't.
WILLIAM TEMPLE

The best prayers often have more groans than words.
JOHN BUNYAN

Prayer is not an exercise. It is the life of the saint.
OSWALD CHAMBERS

The primary object of prayer is to know God better; we and our needs should come second.
FLORENCE ALLSHORN

Prayer is the journey of a lifetime and a journey *for* a lifetime. Prayer often changes our perspective on circumstances and situations, as we focus on God and allow ourselves to be affected by his thoughts on the matter.

Group activity

Look up the following verses from the writings of John:

- John 15:9–11; 17:26; 21:15–17 (Awareness of the love of God)
- John 5:19–24; 10:27–30; 15:5; 1 John 2:1–6 (Confidence about the presence of Jesus and the Father)
- 1 John 1:5–10; 2:12–14 (Confidence in the forgiving love of God)
- John 15:7; 1 John 5:14–15 (Confidence in Jesus' answering our prayers)
- John 14:16–26; 15:26–27; 16:7–15 (Prayer is communion through the Holy Spirit)

The following is based on John's prayer vision. Do the exercise as an individual rather than together.

Place a number in the box alongside each statement (between 1 and 5, with 1 signifying 'always' and 5 'never'), which indicates the extent to which that particular perspective from John on prayer is a feature of your current prayer life.

To get the most out of this, remember: 'Pray as you can, not as you can't!' If a particular statement isn't part of your experience, that's okay. If it's something you long for, then it *will* become part of your prayer life. Above all, be honest.

I know that God is always with me.	
The ability to pray is part of God's gift to me.	
I feel personally very close to God in prayer.	
I can pray because Jesus gave his life for me.	
In prayer I see what life is really about.	
In prayer I am set free to be who I really am.	
Prayer unites me with other Christians.	
Prayer is natural because I have the Holy Spirit in my life.	
Prayer gives me a taste of heaven here and now.	
Prayer makes me strong to face what I need to.	
When I pray I resist the devil.	
Prayer helps me in showing others God's way.	
Prayer is a practical part of being a member of the church.	
Prayer nourishes my spiritual life.	
When I pray I am 'practising the presence of God'.	
When I pray I see and know Jesus Christ.	
Prayer is a way of my loving God back.	
Prayer brings me joy and an experience of God's glory.	
In prayer I'm empowered with love for other people.	
Through the Holy Spirit, I am able to see a vision of Jesus.	

Note your top five scores and get into smaller groups to discuss your answers. You may want to pick one or two areas to work on and ask the group to check how you are doing with this next week.

Day 2

Prayer is about relationship

Before the term 'Christian' was used, disciples were known as 'followers of the Way'. Christian discipleship is all about following Jesus as he leads us forward. It involves having a relationship with God, which by its very nature cannot stand still. Relationships either grow and deepen, or wither and die. God wants our relationship with him to be an ever-growing experience, and prayer is a vital part of this, as it is the means by which our relationship with God can be deepened and enriched.

Listen to what others say about prayer as relationship: www.foundations21.net/prayer

Through prayer God allows us to have instant access to him. He wants our walk with him to be intimate, but, like any close relationship, if we don't spend time with him, talking to him and listening to him, our relationship will suffer.

Reflections

* Have you ever thought of your relationship with God as being similar to a marriage?
* What effect do you think doing so would have on your own prayer life?
* What do you think about the fact that as a child of God you have instant access to him?

Day 3

An intimate connection

Prayer is communication with God. We are able to communicate with God because he is personal and allows us to address him by his name. However, God is holy, and our sin breaks the prayer connection we have with him. Because of his love and mercy, God has restored the connection through Jesus Christ. Jesus has paid for our sins and saved us. It is only through him that we can come to the Father (John 14:6). Jesus restores our ability to be intimate with God.

As our prayer life develops, we learn how to stay close to God. We learn to keep Jesus' command to 'remain in me' (15:5). 'Remaining' simply means keeping on in relationship with God (vv. 7–11). It helps us to love God's family, be effective as witnesses and welcome the work of God's Spirit in our lives (vv. 12–27).

Reflections

- Ponder the fact that it is only through Jesus that you are able to come close to God. Spend time thanking him for his sacrifice.
- Think about the areas of your own life where you need to 'remain' closer to Jesus, and open up to God more. It could be your emotions, your ambitions, your home life, work, church and so on.

Day 4

Prayer is a two-way conversation

Prayer is sometimes described as the act of talking to God. But have you ever experienced a relationship as one-sided as that? Few of us like being on the receiving end all the time. Neither, I guess, does God! It takes two to make a real and lasting friendship. And so prayer is best seen as involving a two-way conversation.

Listening lies at the heart of knowledge, and especially knowledge of God. Listening can be very hard work, especially in prayer. So, how do we hear God?

- Through the Bible as the inspired word of God—often passages jump out at us that speak directly into a situation we are facing.
- Through others and through situations or circumstances— God-incidences rather than co-incidences!
- In our hearts—often this can seem like our conscience, but over time we come to recognise God speaking in our thoughts and placing things into our minds. This takes practice.
- Through words and pictures—sometimes the meaning can be obvious but at other times it may be revealed later. Do remember to test anything that you believe is from God—the Bible is our plumb line (see 1 Thessalonians 5:20–21 and 2 Timothy 3:16).

Reflections

- Look up John 10:2–5. How well do you think you know God's voice? Do you recognise it quickly?
- When did you last 'hear' from God? Still yourself now and ask him to speak to you.

Day 5

Prayer takes effort but also needs spontaneity

Prayer is very like falling in love and growing in love. Sometimes it is thrilling and exhilarating; at other times it can feel more like a hard slog that we occasionally want to give up on.

Anyone can determine within themselves to create a new discipline, but it takes huge willpower to continue when it feels lifeless and dull. Asking God to come and inhabit your prayers and spark life into your relationship shows that you know that you can't, and shouldn't, do it in your own strength and that you want to cultivate it further.

There are times when it will be hard to stop what you are doing and turn to prayer. It will seem like a huge effort. In order to help you, there are many different ideas and strategies for praying in this book, but they are only there as a guide. As with any relationship, prayer with God will become stale if you simply go through the motions of your chosen method each and every day. When you feel that happening, it is time to mix things up a little and try something new to keep it fresh.

Reflections

- At this point, how do you view prayer: as a daily chore or a daily delight?
- Think about the ways in which you have chosen to pray over the years. Do you think it might be time to try something new?

Saturday

Community activity

Get together in small groups to brainstorm the ways in which you can express your love relationship with God through prayer. There are so many varieties of experience of prayer. Of which ones do you as a group have experience? (For example, silence, tears, meditation, quiet reflection, pleading or crying to God, Bible study leading to response, worship, intercession, continually talking to God throughout the day...)

Sunday

Reflective activity

In order to cultivate the idea of relationship, spend time this week really listening to God as well as speaking to him. Keep a journal for the week, and each day record what you hear God say. Then write your reflective response to it. Write an overall reflection on this practice of listening to God at the end of the week.

Review

Over the past week we have looked at how prayer is the way in which we ultimately connect with God. He is a holy God but has chosen to delight in spending time with us, his children. We have seen how prayer can be viewed as a lifelong relationship with God, based on love, mutual trust and understanding. It is important to cultivate that relationship, and to remember to listen to God as well as speak to him! As David Wilkinson said, 'God is not a divine slot machine.' Prayer is not simply about requesting things, but is the way of deepening that relationship of love in the actual everyday moments of our lives.

Week 2
Prayer in the Bible

Overview

There is so much we can find out about prayer from spending time looking at the Bible. For example, the main characters we meet in the Bible spoke to God regularly, and their prayer life greatly affected their everyday lives. So let's delve deeper to see what we can learn for ourselves.

Day 1 (group session)

The word 'pray' (and derivations like 'praying', 'prayer' or similar) occurs at least 367 times in the Bible.

The following phrases can be used to describe the various types of prayer:

- worship
- adoration
- meditation
- asking for others
- asking for myself

Group activity

Look up the following scriptures and decide what types of prayer they are describing:

- Acts 4:24–30 (The disciples and other believers)
- Matthew 26:39, 42, 44 (Jesus in Gethsemane)
- Luke 2:27–32 (Simeon)
- Luke 2:36–38 (Anna)
- Daniel 6:10 (Daniel)

The four 'C's of prayer

Prayer can, alternatively, be described by four words that all, very helpfully, start with a C: cooperation, commitment, communion and commission. In *Growing Spiritually* (Abingdon Press, 1968), E. Stanley Jones outlined the following model:

Prayer is cooperation with God because it means we are aligning ourselves with the purposes of God.

We don't merely cooperate with God while holding certain parts of ourselves back. We need to engage as a total person. This means that cooperation equals commitment. *Your whole being reaches out to God, and God reaches down to you.*

Prayer is communion. *Prayer is a means, but often it is an end in itself. There are times when your own wants and the needs of others drop away as you gaze upon God's face and are overwhelmed by love.*

Prayer is commission. *Out of our times of quietness with God, power is generated that turns the spiritual machinery of the world. When you pray, you begin to feel the sense of being sent, full of purpose.*

Question

Discuss which of these four 'C's you have already established in your prayer life, and which you want to cultivate more.

Activity

Can you match the following biblical characters with the four 'C's of prayer, outlined above, without looking at the text below?

Peter, Paul, Mary, Solomon, Zechariah, Hannah, Moses.

Discuss your answers together. You may not all agree—your view may depend on which part of the story you are thinking of.

Now let's look at the characters and types of prayer in more detail to see what we can learn from them.

Cooperation

Think about Zechariah (Luke 1:67–79) and Mary (Luke 1:46–55), who demonstrated 'cooperation' with God. What did it mean for them? How do you think we can keep in touch with the purposes of God for the world?

Commitment

Think about Hannah (1 Samuel 1) and Solomon (1 Kings 3), who showed 'commitment' to God. Discuss what it meant for them. Now think about whether there is any part of your life that you currently do not feel able to bring into your time with God. Can you begin to offer him that part of your life, too?

Communion

Think about Moses (Exodus 33) and Mary (John 1:21–11). What did communion with God through prayer mean for these people? Have you ever felt that you were really communing with God?

Commission

Now think about Paul (Acts 9) and Peter (John 21), who were both commissioned by God. What did being commissioned by God through prayer mean for them? What commission have we all been given?

Get into smaller groups and discuss the following question together before ending today's meeting with prayer: as you reflect on the examples of these characters, is there anything that you would want to change or add to your prayer life?

Day 2

David and personal confessional prayer

Read 2 Samuel 11:1—12:25. David has been called the greatest king Israel ever had; he was 'a man after God's heart' (1 Samuel 13:14, Acts 13:22).

But even David got it wrong—really wrong! He didn't simply lie or steal but committed adultery and murder. With his power, David could have easily struck the story from the records. However, when he realised he had done wrong, he didn't try to avoid the blame or accuse others, but acknowledged his sin and repented wholeheartedly (2 Samuel 12:13–17; Psalm 51).

His close relationship and honesty with God is what made him stand out from Israel's other kings, and provides a great example of how to confess our sins to God:

- Appeal to God's mercy and loving-kindness
- Acknowledge our sins to God
- Understand where we are and where God wants us
- Pray for renewal and restoration
- Resolve to offer grateful service
- Pray for God's purposes

By praying as David did, we are sure to experience both forgiveness itself and the joy of forgiveness, which David expressed in Psalm 32:1–5.

Reflections

- How can David be an example to you and your prayer life?
- Try writing your own prayer of confession, remembering that when you bring your sin to God he will free you from it (1 John 1:9; Romans 3:22–24).

Day 3

Jacob wrestles with God

Read Genesis 32:22–32. Although this passage is describing a physical bout of wrestling, it also offers a great encouragement for us to wrestle with God in prayer with a persistence that simply will not give up. After a whole night, in which he refuses to be overpowered and his opponent has to wrench his socket, Jacob says: 'I will not let you go unless you bless me' (v. 26). This was a case of simply hanging on. Just picture the moment—it is like a scene from a film in which one person says, 'In that case I'll leave,' and the reaction of the person left behind tells you everything about how they view the importance of that relationship. This was a test: how much did Jacob want God in his life?

Reflections

- Try to imagine yourself in the same situation as Jacob. Do you think you would have had the audacity to wrestle, and then to answer back?
- How hard do you work in your prayer life to get God's attention? Do you think you do enough in the light of Jacob's story?
- Is there something that you have been praying about for a long time? Be encouraged by this story and persist in praying again, even today, about the same thing.

Day 4

Confession of corporate sins

Read Nehemiah 1:1–11. It's not often that a politician acknowledges that things have gone wrong. Here Nehemiah helped God's people to face up to their failure and take a new direction under a new leader. It often requires one person in a group to take the lead in prayer, and especially on behalf of others. We might not normally think one can confess sins on behalf of another, but the Bible shows us that as one person takes responsibility for what has happened, others do too.

You may know about the regular prayer habits of Daniel; he prayed three times a day. It is what caused him to be thrown into the den of lions. But did you know that, later in the book, we get another insight into the destination of our prayers?

Read these sections of Daniel: 9:1–6, 17–23; 10:2–12.

Daniel prayed with others and for others. Like Nehemiah, he took it upon himself to confess to God the sins of his nation. He was bowed down by the state of his country.

Reflections

- Spend some time studying what the effects of Daniel and Nehemiah's corporate confessional prayers were.
- Ask yourself whether you have any role to play in confessing the sins of your people (your congregation, your family or anyone else).

Day 5

The centrality of prayer in the early church

In Acts, we can see that prayer was central to the first churches. Read the following passages and make a note of the circumstances surrounding the prayer, and the effect of the prayers:

- Acts 1:23–24 (praying for a successor for Judas)
- Acts 2:1 (praying as Pentecost starts)
- Acts 3:1 (travelling to the temple to pray)
- Acts 4:23–31 (praying after Peter and John were released)
- Acts 7:59–60 (the stoning of Stephen)

Prayer and the receiving of the Holy Spirit were crucial to the early Christians' staying strong in the midst of persecution. Prayer was entwined into their everyday lives; there were special places and times that the apostles had for prayer. Acts 10 speaks of both Peter (at lunchtime) and Cornelius (at three in the afternoon) having regular prayer times. But there were also plenty of instances of spontaneous prayer fitting the situation. For example, when Paul was leaving Ephesus, he and others met to pray on the seashore: 'When Paul had finished speaking, he knelt down with all of them and prayed' (Acts 20:36).

Reflections

- What new thing have you learned about how the early Christians engaged in prayer?
- Look at Luke 2:36–38 for another example of how engaging in prayer (and fasting) resulted in receiving power and insight.

Saturday

Community activity

Meet together and brainstorm all the different ways in which prayer is part of your life together as a church community. Now discuss what each of you has learned individually this week about prayer. Is there anything new you feel able to try together as a group?

Sunday

Reflective activity

Remember something from your childhood for which you were sorry and ashamed, such as being cruel to someone else. Picture the scene in your mind until it becomes vivid. Now, invite Jesus to come into the scene. Be sure to wait until you are convinced that he is there. Tell him what you need to. How does he respond to you and your words? What do you feel like? Now, superimpose your committing your most recent sinful act on the scene. What is Jesus saying to you?

Alternatively, think back over the last five days and consider whether there are aspects of prayer you have never thought about before. As part of this process, spend some time in quiet, contemplative prayer before God and ask him to reveal to you if there is any new aspect he would like you to spend time developing.

Review

We have seen that the Bible is packed full of instances of God's people turning to him in prayer; indeed, we have only been able to scratch the surface, and a look at any book in the Bible would provide you with further examples. The variety of prayer has also been revealed, such as confessional prayer and persistent prayer. Time and time again the result of prayer has been God's people (individually or as a group) aligning themselves with his will. We ended the week with a little taster of how important prayer was to the early Christians, and how much a part of everyday life. We will see much more of this as we focus on Jesus and prayer next week.

Week 3
Praying Jesus' way

Overview

Jesus provides us with the ultimate example of how to pray. Not only do we see him in constant prayer throughout his life (as described in the Gospels), but he also taught his disciples how to pray, and provided us with the Lord's Prayer as a useful guideline.

Day 1 (group session)

Prayer was central to Jesus throughout his life. He regarded the temple as a 'house of prayer' (Mark 11:17) and regularly attended synagogue on the sabbath (Luke 4:16), when he would no doubt have joined with the rest of the people in the prayers; although the particular occasions recalled in the Gospels speak only of his teaching and preaching.

Discuss together how you think Jesus would have described prayer to his followers.

Now listen to a song about prayer, 'Private Temple' by Karl Kohlhase. Go to www.foundations21.net/prayer for the lyrics and to download the MP3 file.

The song is about going to a private place to be alone with God. Jesus certainly did this, withdrawing from the public for long periods in order to devote himself to prayer (Matthew 14:23; Luke 5:16; 6:12).

Questions

Ponder these individually and then discuss in smaller groups:

- Where did Jesus pray, and what is my equivalent place?
- When did he pray? Do I ever pray at this time?
- How did he pray? Does this give me any inspiration?

Group activities

Jesus spoke and listened to his Father all day long. But even he, who was in constant contact with God, felt the need to draw away for quiet reflection. Luke's Gospel is full of examples of Jesus at prayer, and we can learn much from them. Look at each of the scriptures listed below and discuss together: what is Jesus praying about? What is he asking for?

- Luke 3:21–22 (at his baptism)
- Luke 9:18–22 (before instructing his disciples)
- Luke 9:28–29 (at the transfiguration)
- Luke 10:21–22 (on the return of the 72)
- Luke 11:1 (before teaching the disciples to pray)
- Luke 22:31–32 (praying for Peter and the disciples)
- Luke 22:39–46 (at the point of suffering)
- Luke 23:34, 46 (while on the cross)

Take some time to think about your own prayer life in the light of what these verses have taught you about Jesus' prayer life. What is God teaching you about prayer? Spend some time discussing what you have learned, and how you may implement this, and then pray together about it before moving on to the next activity.

Matthew, like Luke, also contains many references to Jesus and prayer. Here we are going to focus on what he said to others about prayer. Get into smaller groups, read the verses below and then together write a one-sentence summary of what you learn from each one. Then come back together to share with the whole group.

Look at these verses: Matthew 6:5; 17:20; 21:13; 21:22; 23:12.

Prayer dos and don'ts

Let's finish with a look at what Jesus said.

Prayer is *not* about:

- lengthy prayers
- turning a prayer place into a commercial outfit
- praying so that everyone can see

Prayer *is* about:

- doing the work of God with prayer and fasting
- having faith that God can and will act

Questions

- Can you think of biblical references for each of the dos and
  don'ts above? Spend some time brainstorming this together.
  (Hint: many of the don'ts were aimed at the religious leaders of
  the time, the Pharisees.)
- Do any of Jesus' statements surprise you? If so, why?
- Do any of you have experience of fasting alongside prayer? If so,
  share this with the wider group. Why do you think Jesus felt it
  important enough to mention fasting?
- How much are you aware of your levels of faith as you pray
  from day to day? End by praying that God would increase your
  faith capacity as individuals.

Day 2

Jesus' practice of prayer

As we saw in the previous group meeting, the Gospels are packed full of instances of Jesus in prayer. He also referred to God in a unique way.

Read Mark 1:35; 6:46 and 14:35–42. These examples show Jesus praying at the usual times of prayer, morning and evening, but he went way beyond this when he had need. Each of the examples above were times of decision (and temptation), and Jesus' response to this was to pray for longer.

Jesus also referred to his Father as *Abba* in Mark 14:36. This specific phrase has been the subject of much theological discussion. Most agree that the Aramaic word *Abba* is a childlike word, meaning 'daddy'. In Jesus' day, the usual way of addressing God was more formal. *Abba* was not normally used, possibly because it was typically a family word. But that is surely the reason why Jesus used it—because he had such an intimate relationship of son to father. The early church continued to use the term (see Romans 8:15 and Galatians 4:6), probably because they felt the shared experience of sonship.

Reflections

- What is your normal reaction when you face difficult decisions? Does it include praying for longer?
- How do you feel about calling God *Abba* in your own prayer life?

Day 3

Jesus' teaching on prayer

Not only did Jesus live out the practice of prayer, but prayer was also one of the most consistent themes in his teaching.

We are going to concentrate on three elements that Jesus brought out in his teaching.

Trust: throughout the Gospels, Jesus reassures the disciples that God already knows their needs before they ask, so that they can trust him (see Luke 12:22–31). His teaching does not say that people will get everything that they ask for, but that what God does give them will be good. In Mark 11:22–24 he encourages a boldness of faith.

Forgiveness: look at Matthew 18:21–35, Luke 6:28 and 15:11–32. There is an interdependence between our experience of human and divine forgiveness: when we genuinely forgive, we open ourselves up to God's forgiveness and our recognition of the need of that forgiveness enables us to offer forgiveness to others.

Persistence: in Luke's Gospel in particular there is an emphasis on the need to persist in prayer (see Luke 11:5–13 and 18:1–8). Again, Jesus does not teach that our persistence will always result in the answers we want, but rather that we need continually to look to God alone for help.

Reflections

- How much do you think your daily prayer life includes trust, forgiveness and persistence?
- What can you do to cultivate more of these things?

Day 4

The Lord's Prayer

We are going to spend a couple of days unpacking the prayer that Jesus gave his disciples as a template of how to pray. It is a great resource—but do we truly understand it?

The Lord's Prayer can be found in Matthew 6:9–13 and Luke 11:2–4. Let's take a closer look at the first few lines.

Our Father in heaven
Here we recognise who God is—he is personal, a father. As a result, we can form a relationship with him. 'Our' emphasises our fellowship with others under his fatherhood.

Hallowed be your name
To 'hallow' God's name is to recognise that it is holy. We worship God because of who he is. He is worthy of our respect because he is a holy, pure God.

Your kingdom come, your will be done, on earth as it is in heaven
God's kingdom isn't a place, but the kingdom is his rule. While this won't be seen in its entirety until the events described in Revelation 21 happen, we can pray for more of the kingdom to be seen now. Praying for his will also reminds us that we need to do his will ourselves.

Reflection

• Try praying out each of the first three lines of the Lord's Prayer and take time to meditate on it. Then expand on each one using your own words.

Day 5

The Lord's Prayer

Let's continue to unpack the phrases contained in this prayer.

Give us today our daily bread
This acknowledges that everything we have comes from God.

And forgive us our debts, as we also have forgiven our debtors
We all sin, so need to ask for forgiveness. If we don't, it will block our intimacy with God. We also need to show others the same mercy that God shows us. If we don't forgive others, we will end up hurting ourselves.

And lead us not into temptation, but deliver us from the evil one
This recognises our weakness, but also asks God for his protection, not only from current daily testing but also from those trials yet to come.

Some late manuscripts, and liturgy, include the line: *For the kingdom, the power and the glory are yours, now and forever, Amen.* This is a helpful way to bring our minds back round to God's sovereignty and greatness.

Reflections

- Think about the overall structure of the Lord's Prayer. Why do you think Jesus taught it in this particular way?
- What does the prayer reveal to you about element(s) in your own prayer life that may be lacking?
- Repeat yesterday's exercise, reading out the lines we looked at today and adding your own prayers.
- Think about how you can use the Lord's Prayer to structure your own daily devotional prayer.

Saturday

Community activity

Jesus prayed for, and with, his disciples. In the Lord's Prayer he referred to 'us' rather than 'me'. Think together about how God usually works through communities—people with common ground, who are fully supportive of one another. Such communities are able to pray in confidence and act in accordance with his will. How well do you think your community is doing this? What ideas come to mind for going deeper?

Sunday

Reflective activity

Honesty, integrity, persistence, forgiveness, faith, consistency, trust—these are all words we could use in relation to Jesus' prayer life. Before this week, would you have used them in that way? Could you use them to describe your own prayer life? Spend some time reflecting on what you've learned about prayer through looking at Jesus' life and teaching.

Review

We have seen how Jesus not only took on the traditions of the day surrounding regular prayer but went beyond them. His prayer life was indicative of the way that God wants to have an intimate relationship with each of us, and wants us to come to him with all the decisions we have to make, however big or little. Jesus constantly spoke and listened to his Father, often withdrawing to a quiet place in order to concentrate, and his teaching encourages us to do the same, aligning our wills with his through obedience, forgiveness and faith.

Week 4
Ways into prayer

Overview

This week explores various ways of approaching prayer. For those who are just starting out, it can be helpful to begin by learning about some simple ways. Sometimes our prayer life can become stale or needs kick-starting as we've lost impetus, so we need to think about trying something new. The studies on particular types of prayer may give you ideas that you haven't tried before.

Day 1 (group session)

Start by choosing four phrases that best describe your prayer life from the following list.

- Asking for help
- Being still and listening to God
- Searching for relevance
- Catching a glimpse of God's vision
- Putting my faith into action
- A friendship with my heavenly Father
- The body of Christ coming together in God's presence
- Meditation
- A Christian duty
- Spiritual warfare

What does this exercise tell you about your prayer life? Discuss with the person next to you.

Now share with the group how you usually pray at the moment, be it sitting quietly at the start of the day at home, using meditation tapes, praying on the go, using prayer chains via email, and so on.

Watch the video of Jonny Baker talking about the three types of prayer that he uses. Note that he says that different things have worked for him at different times—you don't have to stick to doing it one way all the time: www.foundations21.net/prayer

Reflection

You could try using these three headings as a basis for prayer over the coming week.

- Thanks (for life)
- Lord, have mercy
- Your kingdom come

Group activity

What would you say to any of these people if they asked your advice about when and how to pray?

- An elderly person who can no longer read and is almost immobile
- A commuter who drives to work, leaving the house at 7am and returning at 7pm
- A young person at school who dislikes reading and finds it hard to be organised
- A shift worker who changes shift every four days
- A mother at home with three children under five years old

Many people cannot get started with prayer because they are doubtful about their own faith in God, or because they feel their lives are in such a mess that they cannot possibly approach God until they have reformed. If you can relate to that, it is good to ask, 'What are the basic assumptions underlying my disinclination to pray? Am I assuming that my subjective state of uncertain belief is all-important, or that my failures are greater than God's goodness?'

Group activity

Watch the video entitled 'Prayer' to get you thinking: www. foundations21.net/prayer. Then get into small groups and share the answers to the following questions:

- What have been the best prayer moments for you?
- Where are the most memorable prayer places for you?
- When do you find prayer most authentic?
- When was the last time God broke through to you?

Pray as you can—not as you can't. You need to find the way that works best for you. And remember, you don't always have to take yourself away somewhere. Bernard of Clairvaux once said: 'Wherever you are, pray secretly in yourself. If you are far from a suitable place for prayer don't spend time looking for one, for you yourself are a sanctuary designed for prayer. If you are in bed or in any other place, pray there—your prayer place is there!'

Focusing your prayers

Our focus will change according to personal needs and circumstances, but here is a very simple, general guide of what to focus on during a prayer time:

- God and my relationship with him
- Jesus, the 'Lord of my life'
- The world and its needs

Before you end this group session, spend some time individually thinking about the aspect of prayer you feel is your 'way in' at this particular moment in time. For the rest of this week you will be looking at various different ways of praying—from some very basic suggestions on how to structure a prayer time through to meditation, praying through art, using symbols, using all your senses and getting out into nature.

Day 2

Structuring your prayer time

Many people have found that basing their prayers on the four letters that spell ACTS is a good way of structuring their prayer times. The letters stand for adoration, confession, thanksgiving and supplication.

Adoration prayer is the prayer of love and staying in love.
Confession means bringing our wrongdoings to God, and asking for forgiveness.
Thanksgiving means offering God praise and thanks for who he is, what he has done and continues to do.
Supplication (intercession) means offering prayer for situations and people in need.

Here is a very simple structure called the tsp (teaspoon) prayer:

- Thanks
- Sorry
- Please

There are other creative ways to pray. For example, your hand can remind you of what to pray:

- The first finger, to be quiet and listen to the Holy Spirit
- The middle finger, pointing to God in prayer
- The ring finger, your home, your plans for each day
- The little finger, to remember the weak and needy
- The thumb, used to turn the pages of the Bible

Reflection

- Choose one simple way into prayer and use it today.

Day 3

Meditation

Meditation enables us to take the time to quieten ourselves from our daily life to make a connection with God. Many Christians find it helpful to meditate on scripture, an image or a piece of music.

Eastern Orthodox Christians have long been praying something called the 'Jesus Prayer'. Say:

Lord Jesus Christ *(while breathing in)*
have mercy on me, a sinner *(while breathing out)*

This is done repeatedly until all is stilled within. If other things come to mind, stop them and return to the prayer.

Choose a piece of art to look at and meditate upon. You can use one of the images from Prayerwindows (see www.foundations21. net/prayer) or do your own online search. You will need quiet and at least five to ten minutes of uninterrupted time.

1. Quiet: breathe in deeply and empty your mind of your everyday activities. Start with a simple prayer in your own words or use the Jesus Prayer.
2. Attention: look at the piece of art you have chosen. Start with getting the big picture, then move on to looking at details. What shape, figure, colour or texture stands out to you?
3. Notice: what feelings and thoughts do you notice? What could they reveal about God and his purposes?
4. Respond: speak to God about the thoughts and feelings that have arisen. What might he be saying to you? What do you want to say back to him?
5. Close: close in prayer, responding to what you have experienced.

Day 4

Using all your senses

Prayer is often seen as an activity of the head, and yet there is so much more to experience when we use all our senses.

Ignatian meditation was developed in the 16th century by the founder of the Jesuits, Ignatius of Loyola. It makes creative use of our imagination through 'visualisation'. The practitioner is encouraged to imagine him- or herself in a given situation, 'as if you are there'.

You can use your imagination by holding a conversation with a character in the story you meditate upon, and you often find that story speaks directly to you in fresh ways.

Read the story of the Last Supper in Mark 14. If you find it difficult to visualise, do look online at a painting, such as that by 16th-century Venetian artist Tintoretto.

Try to experience the sensations of sight, touch, taste, sound and smell of bread and wine, the essential ingredients of Jesus' last meal with his close disciples. If it would help, bring some bread and wine to your place of meditation.

Reflections
- Did you follow the method through to completion?
- Was it a success or a failure? If everything went well, thank God. If not, try to work out why.
- Write down the date and subject of the meditation, your prayers, any resolutions and the reasons for them.

Day 5

Prayer walks and retreats

Watch the video 'The Quiet Garden': www.foundations21.net/prayer

In the video, Philip talks about being 'chore-conscious' in our own home, but in someone else's garden we can just 'be', free to concentrate on communing with God. That's the aim behind prayer walks and retreats.

Getting out from behind our desks or away from our household chores gives our senses a chance to have free rein. Try a prayer walk, noting down as many welcome signs of God's creative touch as you can. Particularly notice things that appear 'out of place'—a flower growing up a factory wall, for example. These can be vivid signs of the kingdom—the way in which God reveals his presence and power in the most unlikely situations and places. Often people find they come across situations and people on their walk that they feel drawn to pray for.

A retreat is time out with God, often from the busy activity of life. It is usually several hours or days. Occasionally it may be just a precious few minutes. There are many retreat centres available for day or overnight trips. Due to their very nature, retreats force us to stop and focus intensively on God. They can provide us with an opportunity to reassess our priorities, hear more clearly from God and get direction for the future.

Reflection

- Have you ever tried a retreat? Plan your own DIY retreat package. Find materials to read, to listen to or to watch and ensure you have blank pages in a notebook. Remember to book the time in your diary!

Saturday

Community activity

Go for a walk together in your local community. Take notebooks with you and note down anything that stimulates one of your senses. Interpret the sensations in the light of your faith and apply them to the life of your community. What is God saying to your community? What action do you want to take? Pray about it together either during the walk or on your return.

Sunday

Reflective activity

Prayer doesn't always have to be about speaking. Sometimes I draw pictures or sing to God. Try one of the following:

Collage

- Collect images from magazines, cards and photos that you feel represent your relationship with God at the moment
- Cut and paste the images on card and think about your relationship
- Create patterns of colour, shapes and textures
- Commit the collage and your thoughts to God in prayer either as you create it or afterwards

Prayer through music

- Play a piece of music that will help you to become still
- Silence (5 minutes)
- Then play a piece of music that expresses the glory and wonder of creation or of God

- Silence (10 minutes)
- Play a piece of music that expresses joy, adoration or thanksgiving
- Silence (10 minutes)
- End by saying a short prayer and/or saying the Grace: 'The grace of our Lord Jesus Christ and the love of God and the fellowship of the Holy Spirit be with us all, now and for ever. Amen'

Review

This week we've looked at various ways into prayer. There are so many different approaches, from the very simple to ones that take us out of our everyday routines for specific times of concentrated prayer. There are some that involve us doing very little apart from sitting still, and others that involve all our senses. Whatever you choose to introduce into your prayer life regularly, it is important to add in some variety every so often. Without it, prayer can get too formulaic. Trying a new way in can inject new life into your prayer times.

Week 5
The discipline of prayer

Overview

In order to keep a fresh, vital prayer life going, we do need to be disciplined about it. While it can seem like hard work at times, it does pay dividends once you've cultivated a habit. This week we look at ways to help you do this, and how to continue praying even when it is difficult.

Day 1 (group session)

Ask someone to read the following quote out loud and then discuss together how you feel about the discipline of cultivating a deeper prayer life in the light of it.

Too many people regard prayer as a formalised routine of words, a refuge for weaklings, or a childish petition for material things. We sadly undervalue prayer when we conceive it in these terms, just as we should underestimate rain by describing it as something that fills the birdbath in our garden. Properly understood, prayer is a mature activity indispensable to the fullest development of personality—the ultimate integration of man's highest faculties. Only in prayer do we achieve that complete and harmonious assembly of body, mind and spirit which gives the frail human reed its unshakable strengths.
ALEXIS CARREL

Prayer involves a disciplined commitment, so we each need to develop a habitual routine. The more we practise, the stronger and fitter we will feel. Our prayer muscles will develop to make praying more attractive, even when things feel really tough. It is important to be honest with those we share our Christian walk with. Many of us struggle with our prayer life at times. It is nothing to be ashamed of and we can support one another through such times.

Starting a habit is harder than improving one, so do encourage any in your group who may not have a regular routine of prayer. (Do be honest with one another about this.) Beginning a daily routine can be daunting, but, remember, prayers don't need to be long.

Evaluating your prayer life

Group activities

Look at these statements about an individual's prayer life and put them into preference order:

- I prefer to pray all the time
- I usually like to pray at night
- I can't stop praying since I met Jesus Christ
- The mornings are the best time to pray
- I vary my prayer times

Now here are some situations in which you can pray. Put them in order of preference for you:

- In the early morning
- A quiet walk on my own (or with the dog)
- My work prayer group
- Lighting candles in a church or another quiet place
- Driving to work
- In the kitchen, 15 minutes before the invasion
- At my desk before checking emails

Get into smaller groups and share your answers.

Now look at the following questions, which people new to the discipline of prayer often ask. How would you answer them?

- When and how often should I pray?
- Should it be at fixed times or all the time?
- What is the balance between praying when in need or when you feel like it and just praying at fixed points in the day or week?

Finding a quiet place

As we saw in the chapter 'Praying Jesus' way', Jesus often withdrew to a quiet place in order to commune with his Father. Is there any time in your day when you have access to a quiet place?

You know what sort of atmosphere is most conducive to praying for you. Think about the posture you adopt, too: do you stand or sit to pray, or use some other posture? What do you find is best to help your closeness to God?

Is your prayer diet healthy?

Here are some elements to include in your prayer life. As you would expect, the secret to keeping things healthy is having a balanced diet of prayer.

- Being quiet in God's presence
- Admitting your faults and asking for forgiveness
- Worshipping God for who he is
- Listening to what God has to say to you
- Interceding for people and situations
- Discerning God's mind in relation to your intercessions
- Praising God for all he gives

Be proactive about keeping things fresh

While it is good to have a discipline, try adding in some variety. Perhaps you could use some of the ideas from the previous week, if there are any you haven't tried yet.

Day 2

Pushing through the barriers and distractions

Often we need to overcome our own natural wills and simply get on and pray. At other times there may be specific barriers. For example, Mark 11:25 explains that we need to forgive others so God can forgive us. Do you have any unconfessed sin or unforgiveness in your heart? See also 1 John 1:9.

What difficulties do you have with prayer? Here are some suggestions:

• Falling asleep/drifting thoughts/forgetfulness
• Not knowing what to say
• It doesn't feel as if anyone is listening/God feels far away
• Too busy to pray
• Don't like doing things when I don't know how they work
• Getting bored

How could you counter each of these?

If your mind wanders, try keeping a prayer list or diary so that you are reminded what to pray for. Have a notebook beside you to write down any distracting thoughts so that you can focus again.

A prayer journal can be an effective way of recording God's faithfulness. Write down your daily requests, then enter the answers as they come.

Reflections

• Think about possible prayer reminders to try, such as daily emails from a Christian group or a prayer calendar (see www. foundations21.net/prayer for an example).
• Research Brother Lawrence online. He 'practised the presence of God'.

Day 3

When prayer seems to go unanswered

God's answers are wiser than our prayers.
AUTHOR UNKNOWN

God does answer—just not always in our time, or in the way we expect. Only he knows why. What we do know is that God listens to us, cares about each one of us and knows what's best in each circumstance. He listens to our prayers and sometimes he heals—not only our physical needs but also emotional wounds, addictions and broken relationships. We should be praying for God to heal us to wholeness.

Read the following quote from C.S. Lewis about 'the efficacy of prayer':

Even if all the things that people prayed for happened—which they do not—this would not prove what Christians mean by the efficacy of prayer. For prayer is request. The essence of request, as distinct from compulsion, is that it may or may not be granted. And if an infinitely wise Being listens to the requests of finite and foolish creatures, of course He will sometimes grant and sometimes refuse them.

Reflections

- Do you think God may have answered a prayer in a way you didn't recognise or didn't like?
- What does your natural response to God's not seeming to be answering your prayers tell you about yourself?
- How do you respond to C.S. Lewis' quote?

Day 4

Praying through suffering

Praying to God in the midst of suffering can be hard. Have you ever felt like screaming at God? Look up Psalms 27, 42 and 43 to see what David did in his moments of intense frustration. The Psalms are full of laments to God; what is so encouraging about their writers is that they are totally honest about their feelings and yet then move from their place of despair to look upwards and worship God despite their circumstances.

Jesus cried out in his most difficult moments—in fact, on the cross he 'prayed the Bible': '"Eloi, Eloi, lama sabachthani?", which means, "My God, my God, why have you deserted me?"' (Mark 15:34–35, CEV, quoting Psalm 22:1).

There are verses that reveal to us that our suffering has a purpose well beyond what we can see in front of us (see Romans 5:1–5). Like gold in a refiner's fire, our faith and character become more Christ-like under intense pressure.

Reflections

- Think back to times when the pressure forced you to trust in God in a way you had not done before.
- Write about experiences you have had of prayer and the presence of God during times of suffering and how you could pray for those facing similar situations.
- If you are going through a time of intense suffering now, try writing a psalm, pouring out your anguish and then turning to praise. Perhaps you could ask God what he wants to teach you.

Day 5

Prayer strategies

There are many ways you can keep your prayer times full of life and spontaneity. Watch the video of Elaine Storkey talking about what to do when God feels far away: www.foundations21.net/prayer

Have you ever tried 'praying the Bible'? Here is a selection of prayers from the Old Testament. Which of these prayers could you use as your own words to God?

- 2 Kings 20:1–6 (Hezekiah's illness)
- 1 Chronicles 29:10–20 (David's prayer)
- Nehemiah 1:1–11 (Nehemiah's prayer)
- Psalm 22 (suffering and praise)
- Psalm 139 (the Lord is always near)
- Numbers 6:23–26 (priestly blessing)

Read 1 Timothy 2:1. This verse tells us to pray for everyone. A good way to know what to pray about is to:

- Listen to people when you meet them for their real prayer needs
- Read the papers, watch TV or listen to the radio
- Phone people, especially friends and family
- Use your church prayer information
- Go on the web to search for world needs
- Get prayer letters or magazines and information from Christian and other organisations

Reflection

- Which of the things listed above do you already do? Now choose one you haven't tried before and use it today.

Saturday

Community activity

Set up a 'prayer chain' for your community, so that, as a group, you investigate needs in your area this week (via the internet, local newspapers, schools and so on) and then pray for specific things. You can pass on prayer points via email, text or telephone so that everyone prays where they are, and then next time you get together pray as a group too.

Sunday

Reflective activity

Think about what you've learned about the discipline of prayer this week. Have you been challenged by a particular thought? Have you learned anything new? Spend some time looking back over the week and then reflect on how you can extend your own personal experience of prayer.

Review

We need to be honest and recognise that cultivating a disciplined prayer life isn't always easy. However, if we regularly 'ask, seek and knock' (see Matthew 7:7), God promises to show us his will, open a door on the kingdom and give us what we ask for in his name. Surely that is worth persevering for! While it can sometimes seem like an uphill battle to set aside the time and then to quieten all the distractions in our minds long enough to listen to God, the benefits of a daily prayer time far outweigh the struggles. And when life is hard, we need the discipline in place to help us keep going.

Week 6
The power of prayer

Overview

Often we don't think about how powerful prayer can be. It can align us with God's will, build our faith, enable more of the Holy Spirit's work in our lives and, of course, we can see healing as a result of prayer. We will be unpacking each of these aspects, and more, over the coming week to see how we can live as empowered children of God.

Day 1 (group session)

Start by discussing the following questions together.

Have you ever 'felt' the power of prayer as others have prayed for you?

Have you ever seen the power of prayer working in people and situations that you have prayed for?

So, what are the effects of prayer? If we pray regularly, we will see our lives begin to change as prayer opens us up to more of God, to understand what our shortcomings are and to enable us to come before him with humility. It also aligns us with God's will and helps us to pray in line with that.

Group activity

Take some time now in silence to listen to God. Bring him a specific situation in your life or in the life of your Christian community, or ask him to reveal something or someone you should be praying for especially at this moment. Ask God to reveal his will to you. He may speak to you through words, images or feelings. Remember to check everything you think God is saying to you against the Bible. Then share with one another.

When we pray, we must be open to learning new things from God. Perhaps we will realise that a particular person needs prayer for something that we weren't aware of. Take a look at an instance in the New Testament when God took Peter's prayers beyond his own knowledge—see Acts 10:10–16. Peter was praying when he was hungry and he had a vision of food that he knew the Jewish law told him he mustn't eat. Imagine Peter's confusion when God told him to 'kill and eat' (v. 13). This is where a different sort of prayer begins. As the day went on Peter understood (directly from God) an amazing truth he had never known before. Not only had Jesus' life, death and resurrection made it possible for Jews to have direct contact with him, but this opportunity was also for the Gentiles.

God's active power

The Holy Spirit is God's active force on this earth today. Jesus is sitting at the right hand of the Father, and it is the Spirit who energises us and works in, for and through us.

When we pray, the Spirit enables the power of God to operate. This is NOT a formula, spell or magic. We are asking the Holy Spirit to do God's work on this earth.

Look at the gifts of the Spirit in 1 Corinthians 12:1–11, especially verses 8–10. Which of these contribute to your personal prayers or the prayers of your church?

Praying God's promises

When you pray earnestly, in God's will, things happen. Read what the psalmist says of his experience of this in Psalm 124. Why would God encourage us to pray without ceasing if he didn't want us to be involved in affecting this world? Max Lucado explains: 'God has wired us for his power, but he calls on us to flip the switch.'

Prayer is the switch. It can be very helpful to pray in line with scriptures, using promises God has put in there. It can give you something to stand on when you are in difficult circumstances, as God's word is right and true. For example, you could pray, 'Lord, your word says you will keep me safe in the day of trouble. Please shelter me and set me high upon a rock' (see Psalm 27:5).

Group activities

Start by asking if anyone has ever tried praying God's promises. Then spend some time looking for his promises in the Bible and think about how you could turn them into personal prayers for particular situations. You could look up the promises on the internet, for example, on www.biblegateway.com.

It can build faith to hear stories of God's power at work in everyday lives. To get you started, here are a couple of older stories: www.foundations21.net/prayer. Do read and discuss what you think about them.

If you have time, you could also take a look at websites that show prayer requests and their answers. You can find an example at www.foundations21.net/prayer

Day 2

The Holy Spirit

As part of the Trinity, the Holy Spirit is a person. He connects us to Jesus and the Father, and intercedes on our behalf when we don't know what words to pray (see Romans 8:26).

It is the Holy Spirit who gives us faith and power to live out the Christian life. When we become a Christian, he comes into our life, as 'a deposit guaranteeing our inheritance' (Ephesians 1:13–14), but the Bible also encourages us to be continually filled with the Spirit (5:18). The Spirit comes with a wide range of gifts for us—and we may have different ones at different times (see 1 Corinthians 12).

One of these gifts is speaking in tongues. This is simply a means by which our spirit can connect with God's. We are letting the Spirit put words in our mouths—handy when we've run out of things to pray! Speaking in tongues is not a prerequisite for all believers, but it is one of the few gifts specifically aimed at building us up personally.

Reflections

- How do you view the person of the Holy Spirit? If you have been fearful, why not spend some time learning more about him? You could use www.biblegateway.com
- If you have never spoken in tongues but would like to, you could ask God for the gift now. Many people receive the gift just by trying to speak any words that come to their mind. You may feel silly doing this, but it's worth trying!

Day 3

Prayer needs faith—but also builds it!

Start by reading Mark 11:22–24. Jesus encouraged people to reach out in faith to him. He commended the woman who reached out to touch his cloak for her faith, and the woman who poured perfume over his feet (see Matthew 9:20–22 and Luke 7:44–50). Does this mean that the effectiveness of our prayers is due to how much faith we have?

As humans we have a tendency to grab hold of a formula, but it is dangerous to use one part of scripture to create a formulaic approach to prayer. Nowhere does God promise, for example, to heal everyone for whom we pray in faith.

The central message about faith in Jesus' teaching—and indeed in the rest of the Bible—is that it is important, but it doesn't specify how much we have to have! Rather than worrying about the extent of our faith, we should look to God and pray for what we do have faith for. Spending time in the presence of God (as Jesus did) will spark faith in us as he gives it to us as a gift. And praying in line with God's will does result in answered prayer. Nothing builds faith like answered prayer!

Reflections

- How do you view prayer in terms of levels of faith? Do you approach praying for healing, for example, with expectancy or with trepidation?
- Think back over answers to prayer that you have had in your life. How did those experiences affect your faith?

Day 4

Praying for others

When Christians talk about 'prayer ministry', they mean praying specifically for someone or a situation. It is not a special calling set aside for just a few people. This is something that we can all do with our fellow Christians as we each have the same Spirit residing within us (see Romans 8:11).

In order to do it effectively, we need to remember that we have the authority of Christ. In what is known as the Great Commission, Matthew 28, Jesus said, 'All authority in heaven and on earth has been given to me. Therefore go and make disciples of all nations' (vv. 18–19).

When Jesus sent out the 72, he said that they had been given authority (see Luke 10:19–20). There is an instance, after Jesus had sent out the Twelve with the same remit (see Mark 6:7), when he came across them unable to cast out an evil spirit (9:14–29). The disciples themselves were taken by surprise: 'Why could we not cast it out?' Jesus' reply (vv. 28–29) implies that the disciples did not pray. We must remember how powerful prayer is—and that we carry the authority of Christ when we pray.

Reflections

- Have you ever felt that you don't have enough faith to pray for other people? If so, spend some time asking God to give you more of the gift of faith, and the confidence to step out in it.
- How do you feel, knowing you have the same authority as Christ? Spend some time reflecting on this.

Day 5

Healing prayer

When we think about healing, we immediately think about physical healing. But there are also other types: forgiveness, healing of emotions and deliverance.

Jesus spent a large part of his ministry time performing miracles of healing for a wide variety of people and problems. Sometimes it was in response to the faith of the person; sometimes it was the miracle that instilled faith in them. Jesus showed huge compassion, and the miracles also proved that while the kingdom of God is yet to come in its entirety, it is already at work on the earth.

Jesus prayed for people to be healed and instructed his disciples to do the same. Look up John 14:12–14. Do you think this indicates that you and I should be doing this too?

While Jesus didn't heal every single sick person he saw, and while it can sometimes be confusing when we do pray for healing and don't see it, it is important that we continue to be obedient and pray for healing—and that we continue to expect answers.

Reflections

• Have you had experience of praying for healing for someone? How did you go about it?
• It isn't up to you whether someone gets healed or not: you can pray in God's authority, but it is God who heals. Does that take the pressure off for you?

Saturday

Community activity

Brainstorm together how you would approach praying for healing in its widest sense. Here are some ideas, but do talk them over:

1. Ask Jesus to be Lord over the situation.
2. Affirm yourselves as God's children.
3. Offer yourselves to him and ask him to cleanse your sins.
4. Invite the Holy Spirit to come and take charge of the situation.
5. Place yourselves under God's protection.
6. Affirm that God has authority over the forces of darkness and is in charge.
7. Listen to God for any picture, word of insight or message.
8. Use your hands to bless the person, placing your hand on their head or shoulder. Do check that they are comfortable with this.
9. Anoint the person with oil on their palms or on their forehead, depending on your church tradition.
10. Ask for the protection of God's holy angels or use the words describing the armour of God (Ephesians 6:10–20).
11. Ask for Jesus' healing power to come.
12. Ask, in the name of Jesus, for this person to be set free and released from what is holding them back.

Sunday

Reflective activity

Think of a situation in which you want God's power to work through you (for example, praying for someone who is sick or helpless). Pray for God's Spirit to come and for his power to work in this situation. Now have the courage to do what you feel he tells you to do.

Review

We have seen how vital the Holy Spirit is in our lives—to give us the power to live out our Christian lives, and also to give us the right words to say when we pray. We also need the gift of faith in order to pray for situations to change and to see healings take place. Jesus, and then the disciples, prayed with a power and authority that, as we need to remind ourselves continually, is also ours as we are joint heirs with Christ. We can see God move powerfully through our prayers, but there is a freedom in reminding ourselves that it is not up to us whether a person is healed or not—only God can bring healing. We simply need to remain faithful and pray when we feel prompted to do so.

Week 7
Praying with others

Overview

Let's be honest: prayer meetings can be the least attended meetings on a church calendar. Why is that? Here we are going to focus on the benefits of praying together, how we can approach such times with renewed creativity, and some of the specific purposes of corporate prayer.

Day 1 (group session)

Prayer is not a solitary activity; it is also an expression of the community of God's people.

JAMES HOUSTON, *THE TRANSFORMING FRIENDSHIP*, LION HUDSON, 1989

Questions

- Do you feel more comfortable praying alone or with others? Why?
- What difference do you think there is between individual prayer and corporate prayer?
- Which of these do you find most helpful as a way of praying with others? Put them in your preferred order (1 = most important and 6 = least important) and then discuss your answers together.

1. With one other person
2. In a small group
3. As a family
4. As a church
5. At a worship service
6. With close friends

Why pray together?

Look up Matthew 18:20. Jesus wasn't saying that he isn't with us when we pray individually, but when we pray together, we are increasing our unity. If someone within the group is struggling, it can be so encouraging to hear others praying, and we can also learn more about prayerful concern for others. When we pray in a group, we are in relationship with other people and can ask for prayer support as needed.

The value of praying with others

Here are some excuses people give for why they don't pray with other people:

- I've had bad experiences in the past
- My personal prayer times are good enough
- I'm too busy
- I have other pressing issues I'm dealing with

Discuss how you would answer each of these excuses.

The power of praying together

Read Matthew 18:15–20. On first reading, this passage is about settling disputes, not prayer, but Jesus concludes in terms that are clearly about praying together. What do we learn about the difference praying with others makes to us?

Now think about what you discussed in the light of this list of reasons for corporate prayer:

- It provides a place to be mutually accountable
- It is a place for Christians to resolve their differences
- It is about placing ourselves within the will of God and praying for his will to be done
- It strengthens the faith of those who pray
- Following Christ is partly personal but partly something we do with others
- Corporate prayer can keep us going when things get tough

Praying for situations around the world

When we are together, we have a great opportunity to pray for others around the world. If you are not sure where to start, look at the 10/40 'window of opportunity'. This area contains the largest population of non-Christians in the world, extending from 10 degrees to 40 degrees north of the equator and stretching from North Africa across to China. Nearly 4 billion people live there, including 87 per cent of the world's poorest. The area is the seat of every major non-Christian religion: Islam, Buddhism, Hinduism, Animism, Atheism and Sikhism, and it is estimated that 1.6 billion of these people have never heard the gospel.

Watch the Bill Drake music video about the 10/40 window: www.foundations21.net/prayer. Share what touched you most.

Pray for the countries in the 10/40 window. You can find a list of them here: www.foundations21.net/prayer

Group activity

Many Christians keep on praying for a particular country or people group for which they feel a burden. As a group, choose one from the 10/40 window. Find out more about the country or group you chose:

* Basic facts
* Political situation
* Spiritual needs
* Missionaries to that country/people group and their needs
* Christians and their needs

You may want to write up a prayer reminder with some of these facts and print out a map or a flag. The internet is a good place to start looking, but remember to keep your eyes and ears open for any news items about your chosen country. Endeavour to pray regularly, asking God to give you his perspective and his heart for these people.

Day 2

Planning a prayer time

Start by reading Hebrews 10:24–25. If you were going to plan a prayer meeting for about eight people, what would you suggest?

Here are some ideas:

- Pray for world situations
- Pray for the government
- Pray for church leaders
- Pray for your immediate neighbours
- Pray for particular needs in your local area
- Group the topics
- Encourage more than one person to pray for the same thing
- Use the format ACTS
- Have a period of silence
- Have something to look at while you pray
- Organise someone to start and end the session
- Agree a time limit before you start
- Use music

Reflections

- Have you ever organised a prayer time before? If a group of eight people seems too big, invite a couple of friends round.
- Think about the ways you could connect with friends in prayer even if you can't be together: email, text, online, telephone, setting up a prayer chain.
- If this all seems daunting, start by joining an existing prayer group in your church or go to a prayer retreat with a friend.
- Keep a record of prayer pointers and update them as God answers your prayers. Remember to thank him!

Day 3

Be creative

Prayer needn't be dull! Watch the video about the 24/7 prayer initiative: www.foundations21.net/prayer

Prayer rooms are a great way to get involved with those around the world. You may like to develop one in your church. Find an intimate, relaxing space and then spend time thinking about with what you could fill it, for example, worship CDs and CD player, a prayer wall to write prayer requests and answers or prayers of thanks, a map of areas for which you as a church are praying.

Developing creative prayer events is a fun way to get the entire congregation involved in praying. You can, for example, create prayer 'stations' or prayer crafts. Search the internet for more ideas.

Reflections

- Think about what models of prayer exist in your church. How can you use them more creatively, perhaps in a prayer service?
- Here are some elements you could use when praying with others. Think about how you might incorporate them: lighting candles, using incense, receiving Holy Communion, meditative prayer, contemplative prayer, Ignatian retreats, singing together, icons, 24/7 prayer, telephone prayer links, internet prayer, prayer board, Jesus Prayer, silence, prayer rooms, weeks of prayer and fasting, intercession, healing team, spiritual gifts ministry, prayer diaries, Quiet Days, neighbourhood watch and pray.

Day 4

Corporate intercession and confession

Start by reading 1 Timothy 2:1–4. We have already seen how, at times, God may impress upon individuals to pray out a corporate confession for past sins (see Week 2, Day 4, where we looked at Daniel and Nehemiah). There is certainly a place for this, and it can be very powerful.

Corporate intercession is also hugely powerful. As we have read, being with others can really lift and focus your prayers. In times of focused intercession (praying on behalf of others) you can begin by asking God to impress on your hearts particular needs to pray for and then all lift those needs together in a cacophony of prayer.

Sometimes churches are called to a day of prayer and fasting in order to pray for change in a particular situation. Jesus taught his disciples how to fast (see Matthew 6:16–18) and in Isaiah 58:5–9 we are given a picture of true fasting as God sees it. Fasting is beneficial, as we rely on God rather than on food, drawing us closer to him. It can really focus our prayers, which is why fasting can be so helpful when a church is called to intercessory prayer.

Reflections

- If you want to, go to the cross rhythms site and add a prayer into the intercession room: www.foundations21.net/prayer
- Has your church or small group ever called for a day of prayer and fasting for a particular situation? Perhaps you could suggest trying it?

Day 5

Prayer as service

Our prayers can be about more than just saying words—often we can be part of the answer too. The Bible emphasises that we should put our faith into action by doing good deeds. Indeed, Jesus' life and teaching included both prayer and action. Why do we pray? Because God wants us to make a request he can respond to, rather than simply fulfilling needs. He longs to interact with us and get us to be a part of his solution. So sometimes that means we need to act on our own prayers! When you are spending time praying in a group for those with needs, it is really helpful also to think about how you may be able to help them. You can ask God to direct your thoughts to find creative solutions too.

Watch the video about a woman who acted out of love: www. foundations21.net/prayer

Brigid was forever giving things away, as she couldn't bear to see people hungry or in need. She eventually became a nun and founded convents throughout Ireland, and is still famed for her energy, organisation and humility today.

Reflection

• Look up the following verses and reflect on what they tell you about prayer, and also about service: 1 John 3:16–18; James 2:15–17; Matthew 6:7–8 and 7:7–11

Next time you pray in a group for someone, think about whether those of you who are gathered could help them in some way.

Saturday

Community activity

Together, think about ways to bring prayer to one or more of the following settings:

- Local community centre
- Older person's home
- Local prison/young offenders' institution
- Local hospital
- Primary school
- Secondary school
- Local adult education college/centre
- Theatre or arts centre
- City centre/town shopping centre
- Leisure centre/golf club/football club
- Inner-city public-sector housing estate
- Private, affluent residential estate
- Drugs rehabilitation centre

You could do a prayer walk around the area or arrange to visit the building if appropriate.

Sunday

Reflective activity

Prayer often changes our perspective on circumstances and situations, as we focus on God and allow ourselves to be affected by his thoughts on the matter. Think about how praying with others facilitates this for you personally. If you have always shied away from praying with others, spend time now reflecting again on the benefits.

Review

We have looked at the reasons why we should join together to pray as well as at various things we can pray about corporately. You have been challenged to organise a prayer time with a group of friends and to think about creative ways to pray. There are so many different approaches that can be taken that we have only had space to scratch the surface. I would encourage you to grab hold of any idea that interests you and find out more about it: for example, perhaps a group of you could research a monastery and find out about the pattern of prayer the community has and try to relate that back to your own group.

Bibliography

F.F. Bruce, *Hard Sayings of the Bible*, The Essential IVP Reference Collection (Intervarsity Press, 1996)

Peter Graves, *Living and Praying the Lord's Prayer* (BRF, 2002)

Joel B. Green, et al. (editors), *The Dictionary of Jesus and the Gospels*, The Essential IVP Reference Collection (Intervarsity Press, 1992)

Stephen Hance, *Beyond Confirmation* (BRF, 2003)

James Houston, *The Transforming Friendship* (Lion Hudson, 1989)

C.S. Lewis, 'The Efficacy of Prayer' in *The World's Last Night* (Harvest Books, 2002)

E. Stanley Jones, *Growing Spiritually* (Abingdon Press, 1968)

http://dynamic.csw.org.uk/article.asp?t=prayer&id=450

www.anglicancommunion.org/acns/digest/index.cfm/2013/3/26/Four-out-of-five-believe-in-the-power-of-prayer

www.gotquestions.org/corporate-prayer.html

www.intervarsity.org/mx/item/4638/

http://news.bbc.co.uk/1/hi/magazine/3306185.stm

http://powertochange.com/experience/spiritual-growth/pray-gods-promises/

http://powertochange.com/blogposts/2012/10/06/they-dont-have-a-prayer/

www.telegraph.co.uk/news/religion/9954914/Eileen-Fairweather-The-power-of-prayer-has-helped-so-many.html

About Foundations21

Foundations21 **www.foundations21.net** is BRF's free online resource for Christian life-long learning and discipleship, and has provided much of the material for this book. It's a unique resource for people to use alongside the Bible to enable them to move forward in their discipleship of Jesus Christ.

It provides:

- 12 themes to explore
- 3500 pages of content
- over 6 hours of video
- links to over 7500 other websites
- reflection exercises
- daily devotional material

and much, much, more!

If you go online at www.foundations21.net, you will be able to use more material in your chosen learning style. To find out which your learning style is, do the quiz on the homepage.